Cover photo courtesy of And
West Ham tattoo image courtesy c
Many thanks to Bill Gardner Mark Ward ... Neil Taylor for their written compliments.
Thank you to my West Ham companion and significant other Angela Baldassari for sharing my love and passion and enduring the hammers highs (but mostly lows),
Much love to Danielle, Aidan and little Tyler and extra special thanks to Josh for patiently aiding and assisting me with my complete lack of computer skills in getting this book into digital form.

The author Danny Fenn aka The Boleyn Poet is the creator and author of all enclosed verses.
ISBN 9798336910872

Contents

Farewell to The Boleyn 3
E13 4
A Love Affair 6
The Boleyn's Final Bell 9
Our Billy 11
This Patch of Turf 12
Hammers for Work and Support 14
Claret Skin 16
Under the Lights 18
The Old Place 20
Memories 23
The Champions Statue 26
That View 28
That Bleeding Fence 31
The Cup is Special 33
These Gates 35
The Irons 37
What Makes Us Different 38
Not in Search of Glory 40
Just a building? 41
Come On You Irons 43
A Little Piece of Heaven 44
Six and The Ten (Bobby and Pele) 46

2

Farewell to The Boleyn

Farewell to the Boleyn
Our favourite place on earth
Where once our leader Bobby
Graced the hallowed turf

The Chicken Run is silent
The North bank bar is dry
And as our famous anthem claims
Our dreams they fade and die

The ghosts of Lyall and Greenwood
Always will remain
But Barking Road and Green Street
Will never feel the same

The South Banks sung its final hymn
The West Side is now at peace
Let's hope we take the atmosphere
To the new gaff that we lease

Farewell to The Boleyn
It's time to say goodbye
Some say it was just a building
But it made a grown man cry

E13

Now you've got the Bernabéu, the Nou Camp and the San Siro in Milan
But E13 the Boleyn Ground for me is where it all began
That place was like a church to us, it was where we'd come to pray
It was where we'd sing our favourite hymns and watch our heroes play
Walking out the station, the smell the sight the sound
Twinkle toeing like Devonshire to avoid the horse manure on the ground
A bacon sarnie from Ken to help to soak the beer
Pay the programme seller as you hear the North Bank cheer
Spot the ticket tout who'll buy any spares for cash
Popping into Nathan's for a double pie and mash
Join the queue for the South Bank and its knees up mother brown
As Brooking glides from side to side and Bobby wears his crown
Glancing at the away fans feeling safe within their pen
You'll never make the station is ringing out again
The grace of Patsy Holland and Ludo between the sticks
Little Wardy on the wing and a thunderbolt from Dicks
The games at Upton Park are sadly now all finished
But the ghosts of all our heroes can never be diminished
One nil to the cockney boys you'd hear the faithful cry
Long Live the Boleyn dreams don't always fade and die
I recently made a pilgrimage to say one final prayer
But there was only dust and memory's and the old girl wasn't there
But I'll always remember her at her best midweek under lights

Atmospherically electric one of football's finest sights
Now you've got the theatre of dreams and Wembley or Lazio in Rome
But E13 the Boleyn ground will always be our home

A Love Affair

I've now been in this love affair
For nigh on forty years
It's brought me rare amounts of laughter
And more than its share of tears

She shares me with many others
But what is a man to do
My lover is West Ham United
And her colours are claret and blue

She was knocking on when I first met her
But that was part of her appeal
Her history went back to ship builders
And iron men of steel

She looked quite rough around the edges
And weren't everyone's cup of tea
She smelt of horse manure and hotdogs
But was like miss world to me

She could take me to the heights of passion
Till I'm screaming out for more
Then bring me crashing to my knees
Sobbing on the floor

She could come across as daunting
Especially when upset
But to see her on a midweek
Was a sight you won't forget

As age slowly got the better of her
I was told I'd have to let her go

And on 10th may 2016
My tears began to flow

We gave her a lovely send off
The night we said goodbye
We raised a glass and sang our song
Of dreams and bubbles in the sky

They said they could rebuild her
No need to bury her in a hole
So I now pay her regular visits
But she seems to have lost her soul

She's now dressed in fancy clothes
And I still sing her the same old song
But she now has found new lovers
And their passion ain't as strong

She seems to have lost her magic
And no longer seems the same
Even with her bridges and fancy seating
And that's a crying shame

So is this love affair over
Is it time to walk away
No I'm here forever
Cos she's in my DNA

The Boleyn's Final Bell

Standing in our empty palace
Where the masses used to throng
We'd sup our pre match tipples
Before bursting into song

Simple bricks and mortar
But these walls can tell a story
Opposite our statue
Which screams of World Cup glory

If only we could turn back time
If only we could rewind
We surely would have stood our ground
And not left it all behind

We'd arrive from various locations
But our hymn sheets were all the same
Discussing tactics and heroes
Before heading to the game

You have to let things go
In order to progress
But the move uptown to Stratford
Is Upton Park in fancy dress

So let's raise a glass and say a toast
To the Boleyn we say goodbye
We all know how the song goes
But our memories won't fade and die

This Palace now looks sombre
As we say our last farewell

Time gentlemen please
The Boleyn's final bell

Our Billy

My hero Bonzo
The man could run through walls
When God created Billy
He forgot about the rules
The word swashbuckling was invented
For our commander in chief
While Billy strode the pitch
We all still had belief
With his socks around his ankles
His kit caked in mud
A bandage around his head
Soaking up the blood
He didn't need to kiss our badge
He knew exactly what it meant
When God sent us king Billy
He was truly heaven sent

This Patch of Turf

This patch of turf was sacred
It's where our dreams were made
It wasn't for mere mortals
It was where our heroes played

Bobby strode this pitch like a colossus
Number 6 now at eternal rest
Many tried to fill his boots
But all would fail the test

Bonzo patrolled with vigour
Covering every single blade of grass
While Sir Trevor floated gracefully
Before picking out his pass

Little Devo would drop his shoulder
Leaving defenders chasing thin air
While Cottee and McAvennie
Were an electrifying pair

We'd treat these men like idols
On a pedestal they were placed
But it all came down to that patch of grass
Muddying the boots on which they laced

We'd gaze adoringly at our field
Freshly mown and seeded
And would have cut it with a pair of scissors
If it was ever needed

This patch of turf was sacred
This patch of turf was heaven

It's where we were United
Behind our iron eleven

Hammers for Work and Support

Where do I begin
How do I sum it up
It does exactly what it says on the tin

Hammers helping hammers
Is what the page is all about
Looking for a helping hand
Give hammers for work a shout

Moore than just a football club
This group proves that is true
We look out for each other
In this family of claret and blue

We've all been there before
Not knowing which way to turn
Asking for help is ok
Is something we all must learn

Hammers for work and support
It says it all in the name
No one is there to judge us
We are all one and the same

Claret Skin

We have Sir Trevor and King Billy
And Sir Bobby who wore the six
Big Phil, Ludo and Rob Green
Safe and sound between the sticks

Van der Elst, Di Canio and Tevez
Entertainers who played with style
The godfather Mr Greenwood
And of course Mr Johnny Lyall

An academy world renowned
Where youngsters came to play
Something we once referred to
As the West Ham way

We had a North and South Bank
Where we'd sway and sing our songs
Young Dylan sits in Boleyn heaven
Forever where he belongs

We had electrifying night games
In the wind, the rain and snow
In 66 we were world beaters
When the hammers put on a show

We had Slater Devo and Wardy
Small in stature but big in heart
They gave it all and more
This alone set them apart

Parris, Pike and Noble
Not everyone's cup of tea

But every side needs a grafter
I'm sure you will agree

We have hammers on our chest
And dreams that fade and die
We raise our arms and sing
Of bubbles in the sky

West Ham United
Though we may not often win
It beats within our hearts
We have claret and blue skin

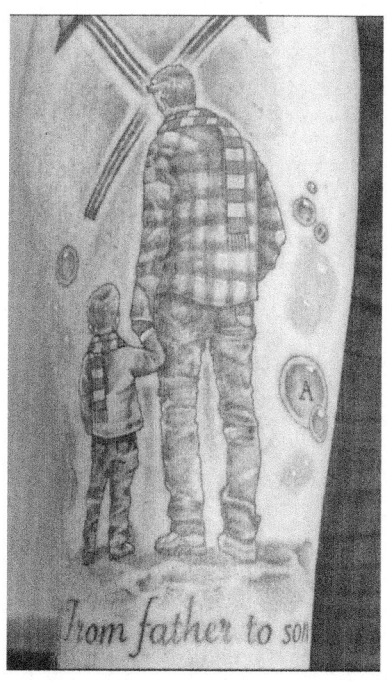

Under the Lights

The old girl under lights
In all her glory
Where every single blade of grass
Could tell a different story

Every stud of every boot
That ever left its mark
The raucous roar of claret hammers
At the Boleyn Upton park

Twist and Shout and Irons
And Bubbles ringing loud
Nothing more heart-warming
Than a proper east end crowd

Moore Paulo Bonzo
And the boys of eighty six
A Scotsman known as Frankie
And Parkes between the sticks

Greenwood Lyall and Pardew
Leaders one and all
We all stood on our tiptoes
When Brooking was on the ball

It was where we stood
Before the days of seating
Who the F###### hell are you
The away fans friendly greeting

You can't rewind time
And dreams may fade and die

It's funny how a simple photo
Can make so many cry

The Old Place

I used to board the district line at Heathway
Back when I still had hair to comb
Five short stops to nirvana
The place we knew as home

We'd sing our songs on the journey
At each station our numbers slowly grew
Friends, family and strangers
All decked out in claret and blue

Johnny Lyalls claret and blue army
In full voice as we disembark
Slowly making our way up the stairs
To make our exit at Upton Park

The coppers would all be waiting
With their vans and horses lining the street
Their dogs looking menacing
Barking and snarling at their feet

We'd pop into the queen's pub
And grab a burger soaked in grease
And give a nod to OLAS Gary
And give our vocal chords release

But this short trip it could be daunting
For away fans it was no gentle stroll
Unlike the modern athletic gaff
Known as the soulless bowl

We'd make our way to our favourite stand
By now we're all in full voice

This is something that you're born with
There is no other choice

Scarves and hands raised high
As bubbles booms from end to end
Unless you are one of us
You could never comprehend

Bonzo our very own whirling dervish
Big Phil Parkes between the sticks
Devonshire literally floating
Either side was Potts and Dicks

Sir Trevor and captain Bobby
Two gifts we'll always treasure
Held in such high esteem
Something you just can't measure

McAvennie and Cottee
Ward and Etherington down the flanks
Unsung heroes like Parris and Noble
Coming through the ranks

Berkovic, Van Der Elst and Di Canio
Wizards who came from foreign lands
As long as they gave it all
We'd sing their name from in the stands

Young lad named Dylan Tombides
Number thirty-eight forever at rest
As well as number six
He's now sat beside the best

I've just took a journey

A journey back in time
The only way I know how
In a simple little rhyme

Memories

Ken's cafe and Nathan's
The Boleyn and the Queens
You have to have been there and worn the T shirt
To know exactly what it means

Priory Road and dog shit alley
And over land and sea
So many who feel left behind
And it's not just only me

Quasimodo and the bloke who sold the peanuts
And Charlie car park my old man
Our DNA our history
The place it all began

The thrill the buzz the anticipation
The butterflies in the belly
When Brian Moore and Saint and Greavsie
Was the only football on the telly

The steps in the chicken run
That seemed so steep
The autographs and programmes
We'd all collect and keep

The smell of beer and hotdogs
And the old bill who lined the streets
And bouncing in the west side
Until they put in seats

Marching bands at half time
The hammerettes who'd strut their stuff

Lyall and the boys of 86 came close
But it just wasn't enough

Silk scarves and bobble hats
Air horns and a rattle
Can the away fans please remain behind
Before being herded like cattle

Parkes Ludo and Rob Green
All secure between the sticks
And those whom were up for the fight
Like Martin Bonds and Dicks

Skilful little whippets
Like Devo Slater and Ward
Pitch invasions and red card protests
To show our anger at the board

The cage and the North bank bar
And the remember Ibrox sign
The onions dodgy pies and burgers
On which we all would dine

The working man's and supporter's clubs
And our statue of which we're so proud
Throwing toilet rolls and banter
Singing bubbles ever so loud

Walton road and Green street
The little shops we'd buy our cans
When we felt we still belonged
And weren't customer but fans

You don't know what you've got till it's gone

Never a truer word was spoken
As I gaze sadly where home once was
My heart is truly broken

Cup runs and dreams of Wembley
Queuing for tickets in the rain
If only we could turn back time
And start all over again

The Champions Statue

I feel somewhat forgotten
I no longer know when we score
My only company is the pigeons
I can no longer hear you roar
You used to come and congregate
And decorate me in claret and blue
You were sold a hope and dream
And ran off to pastures new
I'm a big part of your history
Peters Moore and Hurst
Dreams may fade and die
But our bubbles never burst
You used to sing and dance here
Before heading off to the game
Now they've knocked our home down
It no longer feels the same
Please come see me for a visit
Remember your DNA
When you next play at Stratford
Pop and see me on the way
I'm not going nowhere
Come see me bring your friends along
I'll be here forever
This is the place that I belong

That View

I can almost taste the burgers
Frying on the griddle
And can almost smell the manure
And strong smelling horse piddle

I sense the bustle from the market
And the buzz coming from the Queens
The firm outside Charlene's wine bar
Dressed in pringle jumpers in their teens

The smell of sizzling bacon and eggs
From Ken's and hot dog stalls
Jibbing down Selsdon Road
When the shout of nature calls

Paying for my match day programme
Chat to Gary from over land and sea
Spot the castle turrets
Always felt like home to me

Pop into the off licence
And grab a couple of cans
Wait to give a verbal greeting
To the worried looking away fans

Pass St Edwards primary school
The player's car park and the church
Spot the autograph hunters
Eagerly stood on their perch

Pass the corner of Castle Street
Where once the South Bank roared

Where Paulo a magical little Italian
Once majestically scored

Pop into the supporter's club
Spot faces old and new
All there for a common cause
The love of the claret and blue

Wander past the Boleyn pub
Green Street meets Barking Road
A place where songs were sung
And beer and banter flowed

Cross to the champions statue
And bow to Sir Alf Ramsey's boys
Geoff Hurst and Martin Peters
And Bobby who played with such poise

Join the queue at Nathan's
For a pre match two and two
Or into Cassetaris
For a sarnie and a brew

Turn into Boleyn Road
Join the queue for the chicken run
Come on you irons
The day has just begun

I'd give anything to go back in time
To catch a glimpse of that view
But now my home is Stratford
Sadly, moved on to pastures new

That Bleeding Fence

That bleeding fence was a nightmare
Worse when it was pouring down with rain
It was like a never ending conga
Just to catch the train

Sometimes we'd jump the fence
And duck and dive our way
Debating and picking holes
At the way we'd played that day

Before the stop and go boards
And Westfield's sterile surroundings
That place we left behind
That tugs upon our heartstrings

With snarling dogs and on horseback
The old bill would herd us along
Old MacDonald had a farm
Was our sarcastic old bill song

To some it was a shithole
But it was ours and ours alone
Full of cockney wit and humour
The place that we called home

That bleeding fence was a nightmare
Worse when it was pouring down with rain
But it's a sight that's gone forever
Never to be seen again

The Cup is Special

I implore our manager and owners
Don't trample on our dreams
Don't disrespect the cup
By fielding weakened teams

Still haunted by the ghost of Gerrard
In Cardiff the capital of Wales
Seeking recompense at Wembley
In the holiest of holy grails

To us fans the Cup is magical
It sets our hearts aflame
Travelling up and down the country
In love with a beautiful game

I fondly remember nineteen eighty
Sir Trevor scoring with his head
And a semi-final at villa park
Hackett gave Gale a straight red

And Frankie Lampard at Elland Road
Celebrating like a man possessed
We knew we'd have a trip to Wembley
For which we felt truly blessed

So don't commit the cardinal sin
Give the Cup the credit it deserves
Don't field a team of youngsters
Or the second string reserves

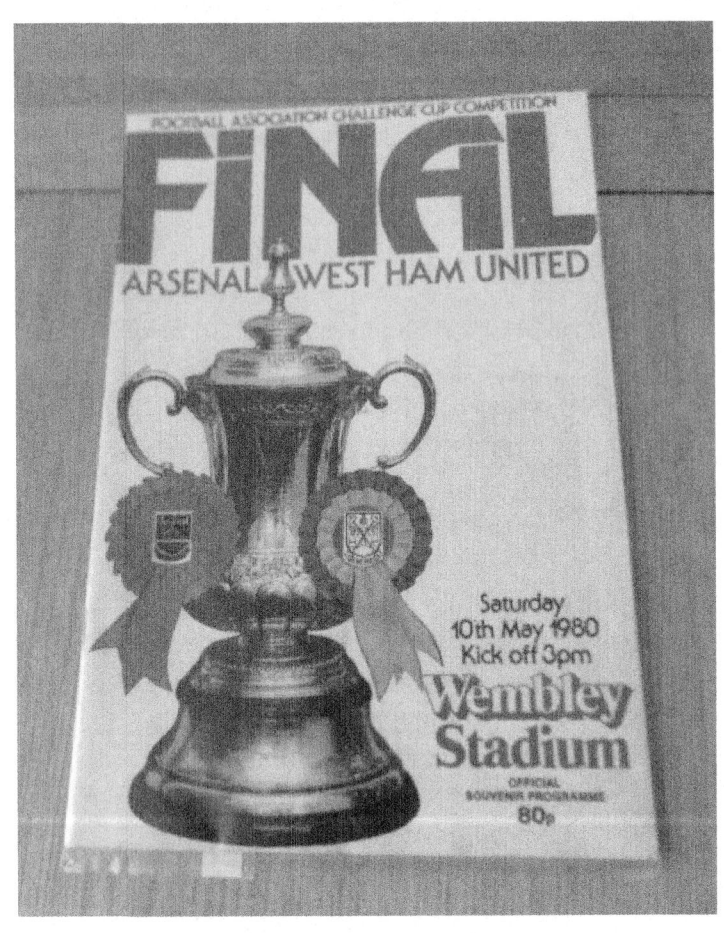

These Gates

The first time I saw these gates
I was trampled by a horse
Pushing and shoving and argy bargy
But that was par for the course

Like the pearly gates leading to heaven
It was the entrance to our shrine
Where we'd sing our songs so loudly
They'd send shivers down our spine

Like our very own St Paul's cathedral
Our bishops were Greenwood and Lyall
They gave us what's known as the west ham way
And tried to do it with style

Set among the houses and traffic
Of Green Street and Barking Road
Full of working class men and women
As the cockney banter flowed

The chicken run so close to the action
Opposition were scared half to death
The west side could be vociferous
Hurling abuse at the ref

The North Bank was our choir
Singing their songs of praise
The South could be quite daunting
Even on the best of days

These gates to our garden of Eden
Where our dreams did fade and die

These gates are closed forever
But we'll never say goodbye

The Irons

Our heritage is ship building
Hammers, rivets and screws
Starting as Thames Ironworks
Now we are the west ham claret and blues

Dave Taylor and Arnold Hills
Our founders from where we came
Starting as Thames Ironworks
When in 1900 we changed our name

The first cup final at Wembley
East London descended in force
The day went down in history
As the final of the white horse

Defying German bombers
We raised the cup during the war
World cup final in 66
Hurst Peters and Moore

Moore Bonzo and Brooking
Father son and holy ghost
These legends
Of which we quite rightly boast

What Makes Us Different

Another fan recently said to me I'm not West ham
So what makes me so different to you
I said when you bleed its claret
But with us it's claret and blue

He said I was confusing him
Could I explain better what that means
I said it's something that we're born with
It's deep rooted in our genes

He said OK explain the world Cup then
Thinking my bubble was about to burst
I said that's pretty simple
Bobby Moore Peters and Hurst

He said I was making up fairy tales
What I was saying didn't sound real
I said mate we go back to ship builders
Real iron men of steel

I told him of the West Ham battalion
Up the hammers was their cry
And how we won the war Cup final
Defying Hitler's bombers up in the sky

He asked me of Cassetaris
And if the legend was true
I said yes mate they'd sit there talking tactics
With a bacon sarnie and a brew

Now I was in full flow

Telling of a lion named Bonzo and the boys of eighty-six
Cottee and McAvennie
And big Phil Parkes between the sticks

I told him that we live it and breathe it
And it involves everything we do
And that my friend is the answer
What makes us so different from you

Not in Search of Glory

If we become rich like Manchester City
I wonder will we change
Will we give it the big un
When the champion league is in range

If we become rich like Chelsea
Will we forget from where we came
Working class men and women
Who love the beautiful game

Will we disregard our history
With crossed hammers in our soul
Or will the pursuit of silverware
Become our ultimate goal

If we become rich like City
Purchasing every player that moved
And if every year we done the double
What would that have proved

That we have the biggest wallet
And our bubbles were flying high
But when alone with our thoughts
Could we look ourselves in the eye

But we're West Ham United
We'll never forget our roots
Moore than just a football club
These rich clubs couldn't lace our boots

<u>Just a building?</u>

Lurking in the background
Once pumped a beating heart
Set in among the flats and houses
Truly was a class apart

Cross the Barking Road
And spot Nathan's pie and mash
The Central and the Boleyn
Join the masses on the lash

Pay homage to the champions statue
Raise a beer and say a toast
To our heroes of yesteryear
And Sir Bobby's holy ghost

Buy a programme and a fanzine
Over land and sea
We had the time of our lives here
I'm sure you will agree

Simply just a building?
But it was vintage like fine wine
When that place was rocking
It sent shivers down the spine

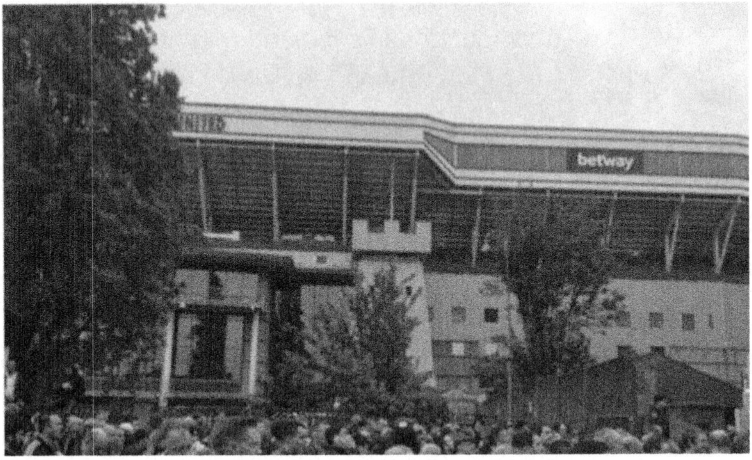
betway

Come On You Irons

We pump our chest
We still roar
Though we are told
We're not West Ham anymore

This is us
From where we came
A claret shirt
A beautiful game

Sir Trevor and Moore
Greenwood and Lyall
A renowned academy
Youngsters with style

That was us
Made of iron
King Billy Bonds
Heart of a lion

The chicken run
The west side
The North and South bank
We roared with pride

Come on you irons
Sing bubbles loud and true
We are West Ham United
Still claret and blue

A Little Piece of Heaven

Has he left the building
What happened to Mr Moon
Will he appear at Stratford
One Saturday afternoon

Is he in a retirement home
With the old marching band
With Monty and Bill Remfry
In a secretly hidden land

Is there a daily march past
Of hammerettes on parade
In a Boleyn parallel universe
Where the best of dreams are made

Does Bobby nod a greeting
At young fans taken in their prime
Telling them not to worry
They now have eternal bubbles time

Johnny Lyall the father figure
Stood at the pearly Boleyn gate
This the Boleyn academy
Where you all will graduate

This is where dreams don't fade
They actually reach the sky
Young Dylan still wears the 38
His spirit still flies high

There is grandpa Ron Greenwood
This man a font of football knowledge

He says you have now left your school
This Boleyn heaven is your college

Martin Peters speaks of 66
Vivien Foe's heart is still beating
Our fans from long long ago
Talk of the west side before the seating

Is this place nirvana
No it's just a paradise of bubbles
Where hammers young and old
Rest their bones and troubles

Six and The Ten (Bobby and Pele)

If I was Marty Mcfly
And could go back in time
I'd love to have seen
These two in their prime

Pele was blessed
With blistering pace
And both were possessed
Of elegant balance and grace

As with all great players
I've often heard it said
The first couple of yards
Were all in their head

Over half a century ago
Bobby raised high
A famous gold trophy
To a crisp London sky

Before shaking the queen's hand
He wiped the mud from his fingers
Now many years on
This humble gesture still lingers

Pele was just sixteen
When he first hit the stage
Dazzling the world
From such a young age

One was from England
The other Brazil

But both were linked
With a gentleman's skill

Sent down from above by the footballing gods
When pleasing the fans was the ultimate goal
Back in the day before TV and money
Corrupted the games soul

I struggle to imagine
Two of the greatest on earth
At today's crazy prices
Just what they'd be worth

Many are now called legends
But that words become hollow
These two legends led the way
Where so many others would follow

Bobby was all about timing
Tackles made with precision
Exact like a surgeon
About to make an incision

Many years ago
I heard the awful news
Of the death of the King
Of the claret and blues

So I jumped on the train
And joined the masses at the gate
And tied my scarf as a gesture
To this all-time great

Taken far too young

At just 51 he was laid to rest
But still remains the main man
With 3 lions upon his chest

Bobby wore the six
Pele wore the ten
Not only great players
But also great men

Printed in Great Britain
by Amazon